GEORGE R. BEASLEY-MURRAY

THE COMING OF GOD

The Emanuel Ajahi Dahunsi
Memorial New Testament Lectures
1981

PUBLISHERS
Eugene, Oregon

Wipf and Stock Publishers
199 W 8th Ave, Suite 3
Eugene, OR 97401

The Coming of God
The Emanuel Ajahi Dahunsi Memorial New Testament Lectures 1981
By Beasley-Murray, G. R.
Copyright©1983 Paternoster
ISBN 13: 978-1-59752-983-9
ISBN 10: 1-59752-983-4
Publication date 9/28/2006
Previously published by Paternoster, 1983

This Edition reprinted by Wipf and Stock Publishers by arrangement with Paternoster

Paternoster
9 Holdom Avenue
Bletchley
Milton Keyes, MK1 1QR
PATERNOSTER Great Britain

Contents

Emanuel Ajahi Dahunsi		5
Chapter 1	The Hope of the Coming of God Before Jesus	7
Chapter 2	The Coming of God in the Ministry of Jesus	21
Chapter 3	The Coming of God in the Death and Resurrection of Jesus	33
Chapter 4	The Coming of God in the Future Coming of Jesus	47

EMANUEL AJAHI DAHUNSI

Emanuel Ajahi Dahunsi was a greatly loved and honoured leader of the Baptist churches of Nigeria. After pursuing a varied education in his own country he earned the Bachelor of Science degree *(summa cum laude)* in the Virginia Union University, Richmond, Virginia, and later the Bachelor of Divinity and Doctor of Theology degrees in the Southern Baptist Theological Seminary, Louisville, Kentucky. Having earlier engaged in teaching science and mathematics, following his theological studies he became Professor of New Testament in the Nigerian Baptist Theological Seminary (1957-62), Pastor of the First Baptist Church, Lagos (1962-69), full time translator of the New Testament from the Greek New Testament into contemporary Yoruba for the Bible Society of Nigeria (1969-75: the translation was still in the press at the time of writing); finally he served as the General Secretary of the Nigerian Baptist Convention (1975-79). His ministry to the wider Christian communities is seen in the variety of organisations in which he participated in his latter years, namely the Executive Committee of the Baptist World Alliance, the Central Committee of the World Council of Churches and of its Commission on Faith and Order, the Executive Committee of the All Africa Conference of Churches, the Christian Council of Nigeria, of which he also became president, and the Oye State Health Council.

Dr. Dahunsi was killed in a car accident on 30 January 1979. This short work reproduces the first memorial lectures prepared in appreciation of his life and work. They were delivered to the conference of the Baptist ministers of Nigeria in the Nigerian Baptist Theological Seminary, Ogbomosho, October 13-16 1981.

CHAPTER ONE

THE HOPE OF THE COMING OF GOD BEFORE JESUS

"What oxygen is for the lungs, such is hope for the meaning of human life." So wrote Emil Brunner at the beginning of his book on the doctrine of the last things. He was right. Without oxygen a human being cannot live, and without hope he has no reason to live. People who have no hope see no point in living, and their meaningless lives ebb away to the grave. That is happening to millions of our contemporaries today. That is why Brunner saw the recovery of hope to be of primary importance for the world of our time and the urgency of the Church declaring its message about it. "A church which has no clear and definite message on this point," he said, "has thing to say at all...A church which has nothing to say concerning the future and the life of the world to come is bankrupt."[1]

How strange that one can even talk about "a church which has nothing to say about hope," when the Bible is the book of hope! It tells us what a world without God cannot possibly know: why the world exists, why we are here, what God has planned for His world, and how we can have part in those plans. And this is not a forlorn hope. It has nothing in common with the classic picture of hope: a blindfolded woman stooping over a lyre, of which all the strings except one are broken; just one string left, out of which to make music to inspire the soul! That is in truth *desperate* hope. By contrast Christian hope is

[1] *Eternal Hope*, London 1954, pp. 7, 211, 219.

healthy and vigorous. It is faith directed to the future, a future which is in the hands of the almighty God who has worked in love and power through Jesus Christ our Lord for our salvation, the God who has a purpose for the future and who is able to bring it about through that same Jesus Christ our Lord. The hall-mark of that purpose and the evidence of its sure accomplishment is the cross and resurrection of Jesus. The God who initiated his saving rule for mankind with such immeasurable love and with such signal power will surely complete it.

We Christians know that God's work for the salvation of the world did not begin when Jesus was born. That event was the climax of a long process of preparation in which God taught his people by word and action his purpose for them and all nations. That purpose, as spelled out by the prophets, can be summed up in a single phrase: it is "*the coming of God* in *the day of the Lord* for *the Kingdom of God.*" We are to consider what God taught his ancient people about these three themes, which are really one: the coming of God, the Day of the Lord, the Kingdom of God.

1. Georges Pidoux began a book on the Old Testament outlook on the future with these words:

> The faith of the Old Testament rests on two certainties, equally profound and indissolubly bound together. The first is that God has come in the past, and has intervened in favour of his people. The other is the hope that God will come anew in the future.[2]

That God has come in the past refers to the occasions when God intervened for the deliverance of his people. Most outstanding of these was the Exodus, when God "came" to rescue the slave tribes from an oppressor, brought them out of the land of slavery, led them through the waters of the sea to Mount Sinai, there made them his people, and from there guided them through the wilderness to the promised land, where he established them as his free people. That became the pattern on which Israel's poets modelled their songs of deliverance. The earliest of these is the Song of Deborah,

---

[2] *Le Dieu qui vient, Espérance d'Israel,* Cahiers théologiques de l'actualité Protestante, Neuchâtel and Paris, 1947, p. 7.

which celebrates Israel's victory over the invader, Sisera:

> O Lord, when you set forth from Seir,
> When you came marching out of the plains of Edom,
> earth trembled; heaven quaked;
> the clouds streamed down in torrents.
> Mountains shook in fear before the Lord, the Lord of Sinai,
> Before the Lord, the God of Israel.[3]

In that description of the coming of God from Sinai to rescue his people as he did at the Exodus, an important feature is included: when God steps forth for his people nature reacts in terror before the presence of the almighty Creator. The imagery is standard in the pictures of the coming of God in the Old Testament, and it finds continuance in the New Testament also. It is even present in descriptions of the coming of God to the help of an individual in trouble. There is an instructive illustration of this in Psalm 18, which gives the testimony of a man who had been close to death:

> When the bonds of death held me fast,
> destructive torrents overtook me,
> the bonds of Sheol tightened round me,
> the snares of death were set to catch me;
> then in anguish of heart I cried to the Lord,
> I called for help to my God;
> he heard me from his temple,
> and my cry reached his ears.
> The earth heaved and quaked,
> the foundations of the mountains shook;
> they heaved, because he was angry.
> Smoke rose from his nostrils,
> devouring fire came out of his mouth,
> glowing coals and searing heat.
> He swept the skies aside as he descended,
> thick darkness lay under his feet.
> He rode on a cherub, he flew through the air;
> he swooped on the wings of the wind.
> He made darkness around him his hiding-place
> and dense vapour his canopy.
> Thick clouds came out of the radiance before him,

---

[3] Judges 5:4–5.

hailstones and glowing coals.
The Lord thundered from the heavens
and the voice of the Most High spoke out.
He loosed his arrows, he sped them far and wide,
he shot forth lightning shafts and sent them echoing.
The channels of the sea-bed were revealed,
the foundations of earth laid bare
at the Lord's rebuke,
and the blast of the breath of his nostrils.
He reached down from the height and took me,
he drew me out of mighty waters,
he rescued me from my enemies, strong as they were,
from my foes when they grew too powerful for me.

This is an extraordinary picture of what happens when a man prays for God to come and help him: the Lord of heaven and earth comes in the clouds in power and glory. He sweeps the skies aside, shakes the earth to its foundations, makes the mountains heave and the ocean floor to be exposed – all for the sake of one poor fellow in trouble!

Now this way of speaking of the coming of God for the help of his people is applied to the expectation of God's coming in the future, and for a good reason: Israel's prophets looked for God to do what he did long ago for his people, namely to bring about a second Exodus, to come again and rescue his people from their oppressors and the evil state into which they had fallen, and so bring them into the promised land of his eternal kingdom. This is nowhere so vividly expressed as in the poem which is in the third chapter of the book of Habakkuk. The poem is of great importance for understanding the language of prophecy. The prophet begins by saying:

Lord, I have heard of your renown,
your work, Lord, inspires me with dread.

The prophet thus has learned of the powerful work which God performed in earlier times, especially of his dread deeds in Egypt and on other rebellious people. He prays:

Repeat it in our own time,
reveal it in our own time,
For all your wrath, remember to be merciful.

As God once came for the deliverance of his people at the Exodus, he asks that God may do it again in this time. There follows a description of what happens when God comes:

> God comes from Teman,
> and the Holy One from Mount Paran.
>
> His majesty veils the heavens,
> the earth is filled with his glory.
> his brightness is like the day,
> rays flash from his hands,
> that is where his power lies hidden.
> Plague goes in front of him,
> fever follows on his heels.
>
> When he stands up he makes the earth tremble,
> with his glance he makes the nations quake.
> Then the ancient mountains are dislodged,
> the everlasting hills sink down, his pathway from of old.
>
> I have seen the tents of Cushan terrified,
> the pavilions of the land of Midian shuddering.
>
> Lord, is your anger blazing against the rivers,
> or your fury against the sea,
> that you come mounted on your horses,
> on your victorious chariots?
>
> You uncover your bow,
> you ply its string with arrows.
> You trench the soil with torrents;
> the mountains shiver when they see you;
> great floods sweep on their way,
> the abyss roars aloud,
> high it lifts its hands.
>
> Sun and moon stay in their houses,
> avoiding the flash of your arrows,
> the gleam of your glittering spear.
> Raging you stride the earth,
> in anger you trample the nations.
>
> You have marched to save your people,
> to save your own anointed...
>
> Calmly I await the day of anguish
> which is dawning on the people now attacking us.[4]

Here we see that when God comes mankind is terrified, the mountains sink in fear, the ocean lifts its hands on high in

---

[4] Habakkuk 3:1–16, Jerusalem Bible.

terror, the sun and moon hide themselves from his face, and the Almighty One enacts judgment on the wicked and saves his people. The language is sheer poetry, indeed, it is intended to be *sung* by the people in the temple courts as they jubilantly look for God to come and save them.[5] It is the poetry of faith that celebrates the omnipotence of him who is coming: the Redeemer is the Creator before whom every power in creation shrinks in helplessness.

As in this psalm, the coming of God is often linked with judgment, but the ultimate cause of God's coming is to bring deliverance and salvation to his people. This is the emphasis of the descriptions of the coming of God by the prophet of the exile, e.g. in Isaiah 40:

Here is the Lord coming with power,
his arm subduing all things to him.
The prize of his victory is with him,
his trophies all go before him.
He is like a shepherd feeding his flock,
gathering lambs in his arms,
holding them against his breast,
and leading to their rest the mother ewes (Is. 40:10–11).

Naturally such a coming is not a mere "visit," but a coming to stay. So we find the prophet Zechariah calling on the people: "Shout and be glad, O Daughter of Zion. For I am coming, and I will live among you" (Zech. 2:10).

Linked with the hope of the coming of God in the Old Testament is the well known expression "the Day of the Lord." The "day" is not so much a date as an event. It denotes an intervention of God in history, generally in the near future, which will bring judgment on the nations which defy the Lord.

The Old Testament scholar G. von Rad has made the suggestion that the Day of the Lord is rooted in the "days of the Lord," when God intervened for Israel in times of war. These occasions were seen as "theophanies," i.e. comings of God, for Israel's deliverance from her enemies. Accordingly when the prophets looked for the coming of God on the Day of

---

[5] Note the conclusion of the psalm: "For the choirmaster; on stringed instruments."

the Lord in the future they used the imagery of warfare: God is described as coming like an overwhelming Conqueror of his foes. Once more the pattern act of salvation in the Exodus comes to mind; for God came not only to deliver the people from the tyrant Pharaoh, but to give them the land of promise; the Conquest was an essential part of the Exodus; so also the conquest of all evil powers was an essential part of the hope of the future.

This explains the imagery which is constantly associated with the Day of the Lord. Its link with "theophany," the coming of God, brought into association the pictures of the confusion of the universe in terror before God, especially of the sun and moon and stars of the heavens. Its link with the days of the Lord of history brought into use pictures of warfare and slaughter. The mixture of the two sometimes led to lurid overpainting of the picture, in colours which often shock the modern mind. One thinks especially of the descriptions of the Day of the Lord in Isaiah chapters 13 and 34, or of Ezekiel chapter 30. But the book of Zephaniah, which more than all other prophetic books is the book of the Day of the Lord, provides some illuminating examples of this imagery. The prophet begins his prophecy with a startling statement:

> I will sweep the earth clean of all that is on it, says the Lord.
> I will sweep away both man and beast,
> I will sweep the birds from the air and the fish from the sea,
>   and I will bring the wicked to their knees
> and wipe out mankind from the earth.
>   This is the very word of the Lord.

If we were to take that language at its face value it could mean that when God comes in the Day of the Lord there will not be left a living thing in air or earth or sea. The Lord will do such a thorough job of judging the earth, not a soul will be left to enter his kingdom! The prophet piles on the images of God's judgment on the rebellious peoples, and later he repeats what he said at the beginning, but with a significant addition:

> Wait for me, therefore, says the Lord,
> wait for the day when I stand up to accuse you;
> for mine it is to gather nations
>   and assemble kingdoms,
> to pour out upon them my indignation,

all the heat of my anger;
the whole earth shall be consumed by the fire of my jealousy.
*I will give all peoples once again pure lips,
that they may invoke the Lord by name
and serve him with one consent...* (Zeph. 3:8–10).

So the Day of the Lord, in fact, ends in salvation, not for Israel alone but for the nations. If it is asked why there has to be a Day of the Lord, and not simply a coming of God for salvation, a clear answer is supplied in the Old Testament: The Lord is a God of holiness; and holiness opposes all that is unholy, and calls for righteousness. So the hope of the future is inevitably bound up with judgment; but judgment is matched with redemption, and so there is made possible the introduction of a new era of righteousness from God. And that leads us to consider the kingdom of God in the Old Testament teaching.

It is a paradoxical fact that the kingdom of God is not once named in the Old Testament, yet it is of fundamental importance to the revelation of God in the Old Testament. L. Kohler put it this way: "God is the ruling Lord: that is the one fundamental statement in the theology of the Old Testament."[6] But that statement – "God is the ruling Lord" – is the clue to what is meant by the kingdom of God in the Bible: the kingdom is not a country that is ruled, nor a people living in it, but the exercise of God's sovereign power as Lord and King. The opening lines of Psalm 99 are typical:

The Lord reigns,
  let the nations tremble;
he sits enthroned between the cherubim,
  let the earth quake!

Because the kingdom of God in the Bible primarily means God exercising his sovereign power in judgment and salvation, it was possible for Israel to grasp that God is king, even before they had a king to rule them. They knew his mighty power to judge and save in the Exodus events; they accepted his rule at Sinai, and they followed his leadership in the desert, till

---

[6] *Old Testament Theology*, London 1957, p. 30.

they reached the promised land and gained it by his sovereign decree. The whole series of events connected with the Exodus, from the intervention in Egypt, to the crossing of the Red Sea, the giving of the covenant, the leadership through the wilderness, and the conquest of Canaan was all seen as one continuing experience of the saving rule of God. So the prophets declared that God would do for Israel in the future what he had done in the past: deliver his people from the forces of oppression and powers of evil, make a new covenant with the nation, and establish his will in Israel and over the earth, so bring into being an age of salvation for the whole world under his acknowledged lordship. The sovereign, mighty working of God which brings this age of blessedness is what the Jews had in mind when they spoke of the kingdom of God.

There are three leading features of the kingdom of God described by the prophets. The first is *the universality of the rule of God and of earth's acknowledgement of it.* Isaiah 51:4ff is a clear example of this:

> Pay heed to me, my people,
> and hear me, O my nation;
> for my law shall shine forth
> and I will flash the light of my judgment over the nations.
> My victory is near, my deliverance has gone forth
> and my arm shall rule the nations;
> for me coasts and islands shall wait
> and they shall look to me for protection.

Righteousness is a second feature of the kingdom of God. Since the sin and rebelliousness of man is a characteristic of life in this world, this is a matter of great importance, and only God can bring about the change. This is what lies at the heart of the promise of the new covenant in the book of Jeremiah. The old covenant was broken by the people of God through their sin, so the new covenant is characterised by a remaking of man to enable him to keep his side of the covenant. The prophet writes:

> "Deep within them I will plant my Law, writing it on their hearts. Then I will be their God and they shall be my people. There will be no further need for neighbour to try to teach neighbour, or brother to say to brother, 'Learn to know the Lord!' No, they will all know

me, the least no less than the greatest...since I will forgive their iniquity and never call their sin to mind (Jer. 31:31–4).

The third feature of the kingdom of God is *peace*. But this is a bigger word in the Old Testament than in our modern world. *Shalom* is the most comprehensive term for the salvation of the kingdom of God in the Old Testament; it includes not only the thought of the end of war, but that of the total well-being of man as he lives under the gracious rule of God, in harmony with heaven and earth, and so in joy and happiness. Apart from the famous oracle of Isaiah 2, where we read of men beating swords into ploughshares and spears into pruning hooks, perhaps the most significant description of the kingdom of God in the Old Testament is that of Isaiah 25:6ff, where the imagery of a feast is used to set forth the joy of the kingdom of God:

> On this mountain
> the Lord of Hosts will prepare for all peoples
> a banquet of rich food, a banquet of fine wines,
> of food rich and juicy, of fine strained wines.
> On this mountain he will remove
> the mourning veil covering all peoples,
> and the shroud enwrapping all nations,
> he will destroy death for ever.
> The Lord God will wipe away
> the tears from every cheek;
> he will take away his people's shame
> everywhere on earth,
> for the Lord has said so.
> That day, it will be said: See, this is our God
> In whom we hoped for salvation;
> this is the Lord in whom we hoped.
> We exult and rejoice that he has saved us.

This picture of the kingdom of God as a feast was a favourite with the Jews in the time of Jesus, and is the one most frequently used in his own teaching.

In connection with the kingdom of God in the Old Testament, the role of the Messiah in the Kingdom has to be considered. His place is consistent with the importance in Israel of the idea of representation, alike of God to the people and of the people to God. The typical figures of priest, king and prophet in varying ways all include the functions of representing God to man, and of man to God. Not surprisingly this thought of representing God to man and man to God reaches its peak in the concept of the Messiah. H. H. Wolff actually spoke of the Messiah as "the form of the appearance of Yahweh the Lord."[7] A similar notion was expressed by H. D. Preuss, in a manner that perhaps explains that statement. He said:

> As in the pillar of fire, as in the Angel, as in the prophetic word, so the Lord appears in the Messiah; not in such a fashion that he is restricted thereby, but rather that he himself, and none other than he, appears to men, as one who has fellowship with them and deals with them, and that in a manner in which he cannot normally be with them if they are not to perish from the sight of his full appearance."[8]

Thus the Messiah essentially belongs to the kingdom of God. Here it is important for the Christian to observe that in the Old Testament, God is typically described as the Deliverer of his people; he comes for judgment and for salvation, and he brings in the kingdom of God, and *with the kingdom he gives the Messiah* to be ruler for him. Such is the teaching in Micah 5:1–4, Jeremiah 23:5–6, Isaiah 9 and 11, and Ezekiel 34. The last named passage is especially clear, where the figure of the shepherd and his sheep is used of the the kingdom. God speaks:

> I will save my flock, and they will no longer be plundered. I will judge between one sheep and another. I will place over them one shepherd, my servant David, and he will tend them; he will tend them and be their shepherd. I the Lord will be their God, and my servant David will be prince among them. I the Lord have spoken (vv. 22–24).

There is a clear exception to this representation of the Kingdom and the Messiah, namely the descriptions of the Servant of the Lord and his service for God and his kingdom. The keynote of the so-called Servant Songs is sounded in the first of them, Isaiah 42:1ff:

> Here is my servant, whom I uphold,
> my chosen one in whom I delight,
> I have bestowed my spirit upon him,
> and he will make justice shine on the nations...

---

[7] *Herrschaft Jahwes und Menschengestalt,* Zeitschrift für Alttestamentliche Wissenschaft, vol. XIII (1936) p. 191.
[8] *Jahweglaube und Zukunftserwartung,* Stuttgart 1968, p. 193.

> He will not break a bruised reed,
> or snuff out a smouldering wick;
> he will make justice shine on every race,
> never faltering, never breaking down,
> he will plant justice on earth,
> while coasts and islands wait for his teaching.

It is possible that the same understanding of the Messiah as God's instrument in bringing deliverance and salvation is assumed in the vision of the Son of Man in Daniel 7. Just as the four beasts that emerge from the ocean are said to be four "kings"who will arise in the earth, representing their respective empires, it is likely that the one like a Son of Man represents "the people of the saints of the Most High," and that he receives the rule of this world from God because he has overcome the anti-god ruler. Certainly in the New Testament this understanding of the task of the Servant of the Lord and of the Son of Man emerges plainly; it is of interest that it was at least adumbrated in the later writings of the Old Testament.

The title of this lecture spoke of hope *before Jesus,* not hope in the Old Testament. For completeness we should say something about hope in the literature of the Jews between the prophetic writings of the Old Testament and the ministry of Jesus, for in this period hope burned as a living flame in the hearts of many of God's people. All the features of the Old Testament hope are present in the writings of this time. The coming of God, the Day of the Lord and the kingdom of God are vividly depicted, with an increasing emphasis on the transcendental aspects of God's works; that is, increasingly people looked for God to come from above and step into the arena of life, bringing wickedness to a halt and bringing in the age of righteousness and life eternal. The continuation of the prophetic expectations are clearly seen in such a writing as the Psalms of Solomon, where the kingdom of God is awaited as the rule of God in this world, and the Messiah as the king of the house of David. This was the popular expectation among the people of the time of Jesus, and it was developed by the rabbis. It was common to look for the Messiah to come for a kingdom of limited duration, and for that to be followed by the kingdom of God in a new and eternal age. This is strikingly set out in the Ezra apocalypse, where it is written:

> My son the Messiah shall appear with his companions and bring four hundred years of happiness to all who survive. At the end of that time, my son the Messiah shall die, and so shall all mankind who draw breath. Then the world shall return to its original silence for seven days as at the beginning of creation, and no one shall be left alive. After seven days the age which is not yet awake shall be roused, and the age which is corruptible shall die. The earth shall give up those who sleep in it, and the dust those who rest there in silence... Then the Most High shall be seen on the judgment seat, and there shall be an end of all pity and patience. Judgment alone shall remain,... then the place of torment shall appear, and over against it the place of rest; the furnace of hell shall be displayed and on the opposite side the paradise of delight (7:28–36).

Contrary to what is commonly supposed, the idea of a transcendent Messiah, such as the Son of Man enthroned in heaven, does not appear to have been an element of Jewish expectation in the period prior to Jesus. The Similitudes of Enoch, in which that concept appears, could not have been written before the time of our Lord's ministry, and may well have come later.

The writings of the Qumran community are of unusual interest, in that they reveal the expectation that not one, but two Messiahs will be raised up by God, the one a priest and the other a king, and the former of greater importance than the latter; the chosen few who are destined to enter the kingdom of God form the people of the new covenant, which in effect are the members of the Qumran community, and with the angels of heaven they will form one holy fellowship. The importance of their belief in a Messiah who is to be priest is a testimony to the felt need in Israel for one who should make atonement for the people as well as one who should rule for God.

It is apparent that there were varied views among the Jews concerning the kingdom of God and the Messiah who should rule for God in it. In due time they were to hear from One, who brought God's ultimate revelation: that the kingdom that comes with God embraces this world and the world to come, the ancient people of God and all the nations of earth, the individual, dear to the heart of God, and redeemed mankind; and at the heart of it all stands the Father revealed in the Son of Man, who is also the Son of God. Such a vision was beyond the horizon of the Jews, yet it is strictly in harmony with God's revelation to them. As in all things, the fulfillment in Christ of God's coming was more wonderful than any could dream: for in him God came in utter abasement to the cradle of Bethlehem; he came in unfathomable love to the cross; he came with death-shattering power from the grave to the throne of the universe; and at the end he is to come with power and great glory in the exalted Son of his love.

The hope of his people and the hopes of the nations are fulfilled to the uttermost when God comes in Christ.

CHAPTER TWO

THE COMING OF GOD IN THE MINISTRY OF JESUS

At the end of the introduction to his story of Jesus, Mark provides a summary of the message that Jesus preached to the people:

> Jesus came into Galilee, preaching the good news of God,
>   and saying,
> The time is fulfilled,
> and the kingdom of God has drawn near;
> repent, and believe the Good News (Mark 1:15).

Two observations may be made about this statement. First, it is evident that Jesus did not go around Galilee constantly repeating these words. This is a summary of his preaching. Who was responsible for it? It has often been assumed that Mark drew it up on the basis of the sayings of Jesus delivered to him; it is, however, the conviction of not a few recent scholars that it represents part of the instruction given to new Christians as to what Jesus did and said, and that it goes back to the early days of the Church's mission, long before Mark wrote. That leads to a second observation: the summary is not of what Jesus began to preach, when he first set out on his ministry; if that were so it is conceivable that Jesus later changed the emphasis of his earlier preaching. Of this there is no evidence. On the contrary Mark intends us to understand that this was *the sum and substance of the word of God brought by Jesus to his people.* It covers the entire ministry of our Lord. In that case it is desirable that we make an effort to understand the summary properly.

Two questions suggest themselves: first, what did Jesus mean by the kingdom of God? Secondly, what was he here saying about the kingdom of God?

After considering the teaching of the Old Testament about hope, the first question should not be difficult. We remember that in the Old Testament the term kingdom, as applied to God, meant the exercise of God's royal power, especially in his deeds of judgment and of salvation, with emphasis on the latter. And that is primarily what it means in the teaching of Jesus. It is worth recalling that the English word "kingdom" has had a history very similar to the comparable words in Hebrew and in Greek. For "kingdom" in English first meant the authority and power of a king, and so kingship, not the country ruled, nor the people ruled by a king. As an example of this primary meaning of the term, the Oxford English Dictionary cites a statement of Hobbes in 1679, in which he defined monarchy as a form of government "Which, if he limit it by law, is called Kingdom; if by his own will, Tyranny." Here "kingdom" is understood as the just exercise of royal power, over against tyranny, the unjust exercise of royal power. This is in accordance with the meaning of the Greek term *basileia,* which signifies royal power, kingship; the same is true of the Hebrew term *malkuth,* and in the language of Jesus, the Aramaic word *malkutha.* Indeed, it applies to almost all the sayings in which Jesus used the word. Think of the prayer he taught his disciples to pray:

Hallowed be thy name,
Thy kingdom come,
Thy will be done,
    as in heaven, so on earth.

This is not a prayer for a territory to come in which God will rule, nor for people to come who shall be under the rule of God, but for the exercise of God's sovereign power, in which the holiness and glory of the name of God will be known by all, his saving power will be manifested, and his royal will – his "good-pleasure" – will be come to pass in earth as in heaven.

The Beatitudes are similarly instructive. They pronounce blessings on people to whom the kingdom of God is to be given, and the second half of each indicates an aspect of the kingdom. Jesus says, "Blessed are the poor, etc." because:

> Theirs is the kingdom of heaven,
> They shall be comforted,
> They shall inherit the earth,
> They shall be satisfied,
> They shall obtain mercy,
> They shall see God,
> They shall be called sons of God,
> Great is their reward with God.

This links up with the saying of Jesus, "Fear not, little flock, it is your Father's good pleasure to give you the kingdom." It comes very close to meaning "salvation" under the blessed rule of God, when God comes to complete his purpose in creation. Such will have been in the mind of Jesus when he preached, "The kingdom of God has drawn near."

But what precisely did Jesus mean by saying that the kingdom of God has "drawn near"? I doubt if any single word that Jesus used has ever been chewed over so much as this one (the Greek term is *engiken*). For fifty years and more this question has been debated, and it is still not settled. Scholars have ranged themselves on two opposed sides. One group maintains: "It means that the hoped for rule of God is to come in the very near future. It has drawn *near,* and so it is not *here,* yet." Albert Schweizer so understood the word, and to him this was the key to the preaching of Jesus: our Lord told everybody that the kingdom of God was to appear *shortly.* Another group, represented by C. H. Dodd, holds that the saying means: "The kingdom of God has *arrived.*" The intricate linguistic arguments by which these two views have been supported cannot be entered into here. We have come to realize, in fact, that there is an ambiguity involved in the language which it is difficult to resolve. How near is "near"? In Daniel Ch. 4, we read that King Nebuchadnezzar dreamed about a tree that grew large and strong, and its top "drew near to heaven" (v. 11). The standard Greek version made by the Jews and known as the Septuagint translates the statement, it "*drew near* heaven"; the Greek version of Theodotian says, "It *reached* heaven"; the New English Bible says that it was "reaching with its top to the sky"; the New International Version translated, "Its top *touched* the sky." More important, in Daniel 7:13, we read that the one like a Son of Man "came with the clouds of heaven, drew near the Ancient of Days, and was presented to him"; in that sentence the drawing near of the Son of Man to God means that he drew close to God and so came into his presence. Is that what Jesus was saying to his people when he said that the kingdom of God had drawn near?

I puzzled over this for years without a satisfactory answer, till it dawned on me that Jesus did not simply say that the kingdom of God had drawn near. He said:

> The time *has become completed,*
> and the kingdom of God *has become near.*

These two clauses are parallel in structure and in meaning, and the one helps us to understand the other. The " time" that has become complete is the time of waiting for the kingdom to come. Accordingly if the time leading up to the kingdom is *finished,* the time of the kingdom has *begun.* A. M. Ambrozic, in a careful discussion of this matter, stresses the parallelism of the two lines of the statement:

> The second member of the parallel can be seen as interpreting the first; it states the same truth. The only difference between the members: the first looks backward, while the second looks to the present and future; the first announces the end of the old era, the second proclaims the beginning of the new.[1]

Perhaps it is important to stress that it is the beginning of the kingly rule, the royal working of God, that is in view in the saying. Jesus is not so much proclaiming an end as a *beginning* – the initiation of that sovereign action of God which brings with it salvation, and is to end in a transformed universe. The royal rule of God has begun, because God has "come" to do his saving work. This Jesus makes known in a variety of ways in his teaching and proclamation.

A dramatic illustration of this preaching is given in Luke's account of the visit of Jesus to his home town, Nazareth. Mark places the episode in the later ministry of Jesus, but Luke sets it in the forefront of his story of Jesus, for he saw it

---

[1] *The Hidden Kingdom, A Redaction-Critical Study of the References to the Kingdom of God in Mark's Gospel,* Catholic Biblical Quarterly Monograph Series II, Washington, D.C. 1972, pp. 21-22.

to be a key to understanding the entire ministry of Jesus to the people. Jesus goes to the synagogue and he stands up to read the Scripture appointed for the day. The scroll of the prophet Isaiah is handed to him, and he reads from Isaiah 61. Luke reports it thus:

> He found the place where it is written:
> The Spirit of the Lord is on me,
> because he has anointed me
> to preach good news to the poor.
> He has sent me to proclaim freedom for the prisoners
> and recovery of sight for the blind,
> to release the oppressed,
> to proclaim the year of the Lord's favour.

The striking feature about this passage is its use of the year of Jubilee as a figure for the coming of the kingdom of God. It will be remembered that in Leviticus 25 the Israelites are exhorted to count seven sabbaths of years, i.e. seven times seven years, and in the fiftieth year to sound a trumpet through the land, and proclaim liberty to all its inhabitants; family lands that were sold should be returned, men who sold themselves as slaves for debts must be set free, and debts remitted. This element of emancipation is underscored by Jesus, in that he conjoins with Isaiah 61:1ff the kindred passage Isaiah 58:6:

> Is not this what I require of you as a fast:
> to loose the fetters of injustice,
> to untie the knots of the yoke,
> to snap every yoke,
> *and set free those who have been crushed?*

The prophet saw the year of Jubilee as a picture of the Lord's breaking the yokes laid on his people, and the emancipation of mankind when he brings his kingdom into the world. This meaning of the passage was understood by the Jews in the day of Jesus. The Qumran community actually linked up the seven sevens of years with Daniel's prophecy of the Seventy Weeks of years that should precede the Kingdom of God; they calculated that its fulfillment was about to take place; they also believed, rather strangely, that the one who should make the royal proclamation of Jubilee was Melchizedek, who would carry out the judgments of God upon the nations "on a day of slaughter." It is typical of the difference between the Qumran prophets and Jesus that the former should interpret Isaiah 61 as proclaiming "a day of slaughter" and Jesus declared that it would be "the year of the Lord's favour." Still more striking, however, is the burden of the sermon on Isaiah 61 which Jesus preached in Nazareth. Luke summarizes the sermon in one sentence:

Today this scripture has been fulfilled in your hearing.

The effect of that on the congregation must have been electric. It is nothing less than a declaration that the year of Jubilee has begun, and the emancipation of the kingdom of God is now under way. As G. B. Caird said of this statement: "He has not merely read the scripture; as King's messenger he has turned it into a royal proclamation of release."[2] Observe, moreover, that he not only *proclaims* the year of release, but he "*sets free* those who have been crushed." The *proclamation* of release is accompanied by *acts* of release.

The consciousness of Jesus that he was sent to initiate God's saving sovereignty is observable through all his teaching on the kingdom of God. Particularly instructive is the occasion when John the Baptist, languishing in jail for his rebuke to Herod for incest, sent a message to Jesus, asking whether he were the "Coming One," or whether the people had to look for another. The reason for the message is clear: John had proclaimed the imminent coming of the Mighty Messiah, who should bring the judgment of God upon the wicked and reveal the kingdom of God; this he expected Jesus to do, but instead of Jesus executing judgment on the wicked, including the evil king Herod, he was spending his time preaching, mixing with people of very doubtful morals, and healing. The problem for John was: when was the real action going to begin? Or was that beyond the power of Jesus? The Lord sent a gracious reply. He kept the messengers beside him for the day and then sent them back with this message:

Go back and report to John what you hear and see;
The blind receive sight,
the lame walk,

[2] *St. Luke,* Pelican Gospel Commentaries, London 1963, p 86.

the lepers are cured,
the deaf hear,
the dead are raised,
and the good news is preached to the poor.
Happy is the man who is not stumbled by reason of me.

The core of this statement is taken from Isaiah 35, which tells of what happens when God comes. Significantly, the previous chapter contains one of those fearful prophetic descriptions of the judgments of God that come upon the wicked in the Day of the Lord; it describes the sort of action that John was waiting for Jesus to carry out. Then follows a beautiful description of very different things that happen when God comes:

Let the wilderness and the dry lands exult,
let the wasteland rejoice and bloom,
let it rejoice and sing for joy.
The glory of Lebanon is bestowed on it,
the splendour of Carmel and Sharon;
they shall see the glory of the Lord,
the splendour of our God.
Strengthen all weary hands,
steady all trembling knees,
and say to all faint hearts,
'Courage. Do not be afraid.
Look, your God is coming,
vengeance is coming,
the retribution of God;
he is coming to save you.
Then the eyes of the blind shall be opened,
the ears of the deaf unsealed,
then the lame shall leap like a deer
and the tongues of the dumb sing for joy.

This passage speaks of the coming of God for his people's salvation; as the heavens and the earth shudder before his coming for judgment, so all nature rejoices and bursts into fruitfulness at his coming for salvation. The implication of the citation by Jesus is plain: God comes to people in the ministry of Jesus, and through him the deliverance and transformation of the new age is taking place in accordance with the promise.

After John's messengers had departed, Jesus paid a tribute

to John, but he added an enigmatic statement which has puzzled translators. The AV, the RSV and the NEB all translate Matthew 11:12 more or less in the same way:

> From the days of John the Baptist until now
> the kingdom of heaven has suffered violence,
> and violent men are taking it by force.

Nevertheless the NEB and the RSV both given an alternative translation in the second line, which I observe has been adopted in the text of the NIV:

> From the days of John the Baptist until now
> the kingdom of heaven *has been coming violently...*

On investigating the Hebrew and Aramaic terms assumed in the Greek text of our gospels, it appears to me that an identical word has been used by Jesus in the second and third lines, which makes a word-play possible, like this:

> From the days of John the Baptist until now
> the kingdom of heaven has made a powerful breach into
>   the world,
> and violent men are making a powerful assault upon it.

This process of the kingdom powerfully breaking into the world and of its being powerfully resisted has been taking place in the ministry of both John and Jesus; the resistance is manifest in that John is imprisoned and is facing death, and Jesus is opposed by various factions within Israel, to say nothing of demonic powers. It would appear that three periods are here distinguished by our Lord: the period of law and prophets, preceding the kingdom of God; the time of John's ministry, which served as an introduction to the period of God's kingly work; and the ministry of Jesus, in which God is at work in great power. This work of the kingdom is being strongly resisted; as John was eliminated, so the attempt will be made to eliminate Jesus also; but in the end the kingdom must prevail.

Something akin to this teaching was spoken by Jesus to certain Pharisees, who alleged that his extraordinary works are to be explained by his being in league with the devil. Jesus replied by a parable, and then by plain statement:

> No one can break into a strong man's house and make off with
> his goods unless he has first tied the strong man up; then he can

ransack the house (Mark 3:27).

The elements of this picture are reminiscent of several Old Testament passages, especially of Isaiah 49:24ff:

> Can plunder be taken from warriors,
> or captives rescued from the fierce?
> This is what the Lord says:
> "Yes, captives will be taken from warriors,
> and plunder retrieved from the fierce;
> I will contend with those who contend with you,
> and your children I will save...
> Then all mankind will know
> that I, the Lord, am your Saviour,
> your Redeemer, the Mighty One of Jacob."

The language of Jesus implies that the "strong man" has already been defeated by one stronger than he. He has "tied up" the strong man, and so is releasing his captives; but the victory and the release of the captives are on God's behalf, and are achieved as his agent. It is the mighty power of God at work in Jesus which is setting free the captives of the devil; and that is another indication of the coming of God in his saving kingdom in the works of Jesus.

This is confirmed in the plain statement of Matthew 12:28, set by Matthew in the same context as the parable. In contrast to the allegations that the power of evil was the inspiration of Jesus' works, Jesus replies:

> If it is by the Spirit of God that I drive out the demons, then be sure that the kingdom of God has already come upon you.

No clearer statement of the presence of the powerful and saving rule of God at work in Jesus occurs in the Gospels. Ernst Percy briefly summed up its message: "Where Satan is driven back, the rule of God begins."[3] T. W. Manson cited Arbesmann's description of the elaborate preparations which were made in the Gentile world of Jesus' day to enable men to get into contact with the gods; Porphyry is quoted as saying, "When the evil demons have departed, the coming of the god may take place." On that Manson commented:

> This is in sharp contrast with our text, where the exit of the evil spirits is the result of the Divine presence, not the preparation

---

[3] *Die Botschaft Jesu*, Lunds Universitet Arsskrift, N.F. Avd.i, Band 49, Nr. 5, P. 179.

for it. This is the difference between the gospel and other religions.[4]

In the working of Jesus, the living God himself has drawn near, and his sovereign saving power is operative in and through him.

One further saying of Jesus we would adduce in this discussion. When he was asked by Pharisees when the kingdom of God was coming he stated: "The kingdom of God does not come by observation," by which he meant that its coming cannot be calculated by observing and fixing signs, whether through observing the movements of sun or moon or stars or happenings on earth. Rather, Jesus said, "The kingdom of God is..." Where? The traditional interpretation of Jesus' words is, "*within you*," yet that is a doubtful understanding; for apart from the fact that Jesus was apparently addressing unbelieving Pharisees, God's reign is not simply within the hearts of men, but includes the totality of life and embraces the universe itself. Did Jesus, then, mean that the kingdom of God is "*among* you"? That would make excellent sense, and would imply that its presence among them was because it was at work in and through Jesus. But the translation of the term *entos* by "among" is, to say the least, infrequently attested. More recently scholars are coming to believe that Jesus meant, "The kingdom of God is *within your reach*"; that is, it is within the power of his hearers to enter it and secure its blessings, because God's saving rule had come among men in and through Jesus; his questioners had but to give up their opposition to Jesus and respond to the message that he brought and they, too, would experience the saving power of God. We are reminded of the answer Jesus gave to an unnamed questioner who asked him, "Lord, are only a few people going to be saved?" He replied: "Make every effort to enter through the narrow door, because many, I tell you, will try to enter and will not be able to" (Luke 13:23–24). In other words: "Whether there be many or few, make sure you are one of those who will be saved!" The coming of God in Jesus was not intended to enable people to answer theological puzzles, but to present them with the opportunity of entering

---

[4] *The Sayings of Jesus*, London 1949, p. 86.

the eternal kingdom, and that calls for the decision of faith.

Now that last observation raises a question, which at some time everyone must face when pondering the teaching of Jesus: What does all this instruction about the kingdom of God imply concerning the relation of Jesus to that Kingdom? Mark 1:15 presents Jesus as the herald of the kingdom of God, but clearly he is so in a sense that holds good of no prophet, not even of John the Baptist, who was the culmination of all prophets, for in Jesus God's saving rule is unprecedentedly at work among men. If John shares with Jesus the sacred task of introducing the time of God's sovereignty, it powerfully thrusts forward in Jesus, as the effective *Initiator* of the kingdom of God. As the conqueror of Satan he is, we may say, the *Champion* of the kingdom of God against the great opponent, setting men free from his bondage. Since Jesus casts out demons by the Spirit of God, the kingdom of God is "upon" men; he, then, is the *Instrument* of God's saving rule. If in the activity of Jesus, the kingdom of God is in the midst of men, making it within their grasp to receive its blessings, he may be viewed as the *Representative* of the kingdom of God. If the miracles of the new age are performed through Jesus, in fulfillment of the ancient prophecies, then he may be seen as the *Bearer* of the kingdom of God, or its *Mediator*. To his disciples Jesus said, "To you the secret of the kingdom of God has been given"; for he is the *Revealer* of the rule of God.

What name then shall we give to him who is as the Initiator of the kingdom of God, Champion of the kingdom, Instrument of the kingdom, Representative of the kingdom, Mediator of the kingdom, Bearer of the kingdom, Revealer of the kingdom? Shall we call him the Messiah? The chief difference between Jesus in the gospels and the Messiah in the Old Testament is that, in the latter the Messiah is not typically understood as the agent through whom the kingdom of God comes, but as the representative of the kingdom when God establishes it. God comes in his almighty power to judge and to save, and in bestowing the kingdom he gives the Messiah also. The major presupposition of the teaching of Jesus about the kingdom of God, however, is that in his total ministry God is present, bringing the kingdom in and through him. If therefore "Messiah" is an inadequate term to convey all that Jesus is in relation to the kingdom of God, at least nothing less than that will do to describe him.

Ernst Fuchs, when commenting on the parables of the Lost Sheep, the Lost Coin, and the Lost Sons, wherein Jesus defended his conduct, particularly his association with those beyond the pale of respectable society, made the following observation:

> We are confronted by a very daring line of conduct on the part of Jesus: *he dares to affirm the will of God as though he himself stood in God's place.*[5]

The defence of Jesus as to his ways is a revelation of God in his saving sovereignty, expounded in words and deeds of saving love. That is why he concluded his message to John the Baptist: "Happy is the man who does not find me a stumbling block." For to recognize in Jesus the revelation of the kingdom of God is to find the way into the kingdom; to stumble at him is to stumble into ruin. There was the best of reasons for a later follower of Jesus to describe him as "the one Mediator between God and man, the man Christ Jesus." *That* he proved to be in the foundation of the kingdom of God. *That* he ever remains.

---

[5] *Studies of the Historical Jesus,* in Studies in Biblical Theology no. 42, London 1964, pp. 153f.

CHAPTER THREE

THE COMING OF GOD IN THE DEATH AND RESURRECTION OF JESUS

In the previous chapter we saw that Jesus both proclaimed the kingdom of God to his generation and was the instrument of its coming to them. In his ministry of powerful word and deed God was present, fulfilling the promise that he would come and establish his saving sovereignty among his people, and so for all the world. Now it is equally evident from the records of our Lord's teaching and action that he believed that he was called of God to give his life on behalf of his people, and indeed for all. The question arises: How did Jesus relate his mission to bring the kingdom of God to mankind with his vocation to suffer for mankind?

Two answers have been given to this question, consistent with the presuppositions of those who gave them. Albert Schweitzer believed that Jesus looked for God's kingdom to come in the immediate future; quite specifically, he expected it to come during his disciples' mission to Israel (Matthew 10:23). The cataclysmic end of all things did not occur at that time. What, then, stopped it from coming? Schweitzer gave a simple answer: according to the Bible and current Jewish teaching, the Day of the Lord, or the tribulation of the end-time, precedes the kingdom of God; Jesus therefore determined to bear this tribulation himself, and so bring the kingdom to man. Of this supposed conviction of Jesus, Schweitzer wrote:

> In the secret of his passion which Jesus reveals to the disciples at Caesarea Philippi, the pre-Messianic tribulation is for others set

aside, abolished, concentrated upon himself alone, and that in the form that they are fulfilled in his own passion and death at Jerusalem. That was the new conviction that had dawned upon him. *He must suffer for others... that the kingdom might come.*[1]

C. H. Dodd found that answer unacceptable. In his view Jesus proclaimed that the kingdom of God had come, and it was revealed in his miracles of deliverance; if the kingdom was already present among men, how should Jesus suffer that the kingdom might come through his death? Dodd, therefore, on the basis of his interpretation of the teaching of Jesus on the kingdom, saw the death of Jesus as falling *within* the kingdom of God. The death of Jesus is a revelation of God's victory over sin, just as the exorcisms are revelations of God's victory over the power of the devil. Jesus' death thus reveals the love of God that seeks sinners and the righteousness of God that redeems them. Judgment and salvation, said Dodd, are functions of the kingdom of God, not its antecedents; that is to say, judgment and salvation do not go before the kingdom of God, rather they are actions which reveal God's presence, working in sovereign power to remove sin and to make God's righteousness and life triumphant; they are therefore evidences of the kingdom of God in the world, not anticipations of it.[2]

These opposing views could appear as very puzzling, for there is much to be said for both of them. I suggest therefore a simpler interpretation, which does justice to the concerns which these two writers had in view: *Jesus is the Mediator of the kingdom of God to man in the totality of his action for man,* and this includes his ministry, his dying, his rising, and even his coming again at the end of the age. God's saving rule expresses itself in many ways, and in the ministry of Jesus we see many aspects of that rule; its supreme revelation took place in the climax of his service for God and man, namely in his death and resurrection; but all these acts are also to be seen as the sovereign action of God in Christ for the salvation of the world. We shall turn our attention to some of the utterances of Jesus in which this truth appears to be expressed.

[1] *The Quest of the Historical Jesus,* London 2nd ed. 1911, pp. 386-7.
[2] *The Parables of the Kingdom,* London 2nd ed. 1936, pp. 75-80.

CHAPTER THREE

THE COMING OF GOD IN THE DEATH AND RESURRECTION OF JESUS

In the previous chapter we saw that Jesus both proclaimed the kingdom of God to his generation and was the instrument of its coming to them. In his ministry of powerful word and deed God was present, fulfilling the promise that he would come and establish his saving sovereignty among his people, and so for all the world. Now it is equally evident from the records of our Lord's teaching and action that he believed that he was called of God to give his life on behalf of his people, and indeed for all. The question arises: How did Jesus relate his mission to bring the kingdom of God to mankind with his vocation to suffer for mankind?

Two answers have been given to this question, consistent with the presuppositions of those who gave them. Albert Schweitzer believed that Jesus looked for God's kingdom to come in the immediate future; quite specifically, he expected it to come during his disciples' mission to Israel (Matthew 10:23). The cataclysmic end of all things did not occur at that time. What, then, stopped it from coming? Schweitzer gave a simple answer: according to the Bible and current Jewish teaching, the Day of the Lord, or the tribulation of the end-time, precedes the kingdom of God; Jesus therefore determined to bear this tribulation himself, and so bring the kingdom to man. Of this supposed conviction of Jesus, Schweitzer wrote:

> In the secret of his passion which Jesus reveals to the disciples at Caesarea Philippi, the pre-Messianic tribulation is for others set

aside, abolished, concentrated upon himself alone, and that in the form that they are fulfilled in his own passion and death at Jerusalem. That was the new conviction that had dawned upon him. *He must suffer for others... that the kingdom might come.*[1] C. H. Dodd found that answer unacceptable. In his view Jesus proclaimed that the kingdom of God had come, and it was revealed in his miracles of deliverance; if the kingdom was already present among men, how should Jesus suffer that the kingdom might come through his death? Dodd, therefore, on the basis of his interpretation of the teaching of Jesus on the kingdom, saw the death of Jesus as falling *within* the kingdom of God. The death of Jesus is a revelation of God's victory over sin, just as the exorcisms are revelations of God's victory over the power of the devil. Jesus' death thus reveals the love of God that seeks sinners and the righteousness of God that redeems them. Judgment and salvation, said Dodd, are functions of the kingdom of God, not its antecedents; that is to say, judgment and salvation do not go before the kingdom of God, rather they are actions which reveal God's presence, working in sovereign power to remove sin and to make God's righteousness and life triumphant; they are therefore evidences of the kingdom of God in the world, not anticipations of it.[2]

These opposing views could appear as very puzzling, for there is much to be said for both of them. I suggest therefore a simpler interpretation, which does justice to the concerns which these two writers had in view: *Jesus is the Mediator of the kingdom of God to man in the totality of his action for man,* and this includes his ministry, his dying, his rising, and even his coming again at the end of the age. God's saving rule expresses itself in many ways, and in the ministry of Jesus we see many aspects of that rule; its supreme revelation took place in the climax of his service for God and man, namely in his death and resurrection; but all these acts are also to be seen as the sovereign action of God in Christ for the salvation of the world. We shall turn our attention to some of the utterances of Jesus in which this truth appears to be expressed.

[1] *The Quest of the Historical Jesus,* London 2nd ed. 1911, pp. 386-7.
[2] *The Parables of the Kingdom,* London 2nd ed. 1936, pp. 75-80.

Peter's confession of Jesus as the Messiah is followed in Mark by the first of three so-called "predictions of the passion" – prophecies of the suffering and death which Jesus saw ahead of him. The passages in which these occur are easily remembered: Mark 8:31, 9:31, 10:32. Despite their differences of wording they are bound together by a common content: they speak not simply of Jesus suffering, but of the Son of Man who will suffer; he is destined to be killed, but afterwards to be raised to life, and this last event will take place "after three days." This expression "after three days" is surprising, for in the earliest preaching of the gospel the resurrection of Jesus is always spoken of as happening "on the third day," and in Matthew and Luke that phrase appears in the predictions of the passion. It is now recognized that there is no difference in meaning between the two expressions, since the Jewish mode of counting days included the first and last; but the fact that Mark did not use the common Christian way of speaking about the resurrection, but employed this unusual expression, hints that he found it in his source of the sayings and that he stuck to it. It suggests that Mark kept closely to his source of information about the sufferings and death of Jesus.

The first statement in Mark 8:31 reads:

> The Son of Man must suffer many things, and be rejected by the elders and the chief priests and the scribes, and be killed, and after three days rise again.

The opening words of the saying have raised a difficulty for some critical writers: "The Son of Man *must* suffer." There is no word for "must" in the language which Jesus spoke (Aramaic). The term in our Greek gospels is well known – *dei*; but it has no equivalent in Aramaic. Scholars point out that this same term occurs in the Greek version of Daniel 2:28, where the Aramaic original says that God has shown King Nebuchadnezzar "what *will* happen in days to come," but the Greek translation renders it, "what *must* happen in days to come." It has been maintained, therefore, that the saying in Mark 8:31 must have originated in a church which read the Bible only in Greek, and which did not know the language of Jesus; he could not have said it himself, so the words will have been placed in his mouth by an unknown Greek-speaking teacher.

People who have so spoken should have looked a bit further than Daniel 2:28. For that word *dei*, must, occurs again in the very next sentence, Daniel 2:29, for a simple future; and in v.45, the Greek version of Theodotion uses the word "must," whereas the Septuagint has a simple future. There is evidently a certain interchangeability in the use of the word "must" and the future tense, and the same thing is observable in the gospels themselves. There is a simple reason for this: when the Bible, Old Testament and New Testament, talks about things that are to come to pass in the purpose of God, there is a tendency of translators to use the word "must" instead of an ordinary future verb, in the conviction that when God says that a thing is going to come to pass it *must* come to pass! A similar kind of thing is standard in translating the Bible into English. Our language distinguishes between "shall" and "will" when speaking of things that relate to the future; "I *will* go" is emphatic ("You may not like it, and you may try to stop me, but I *will* go, whatever you say or do!"); but we reverse the application in the third person: "he will go" is unemphatic, "he shall go" is emphatic. People frequently get mixed up in their use of these words, but Bible translators do not, and from the King James Version to the New International Version this distinction is observed in putting the Bible into English. The lesson to be drawn regarding Mark 8:31 is clear: whoever passed on that saying knew how to put the language of the Old Testament and the language of Jesus into Greek; Rudolph Pesch suggested that the person could well have been in the church of Jerusalem, where the Bible was read in Hebrew, where Aramaic was spoken, and where Greek-speaking synagogues existed and Greek-speaking Christian Jews like Stephen lived and worked.[3] So there's no reason on the score of language why Jesus should not have said Mark 8:31.

The second passion prediction, Mark 9:31, uses a significantly different verb: "The Son of Man will be delivered into

---

[3] *Die Passion des Menschensohnes*, in *Jesus und der Menschensohn*, ed. R. Pesch and R. Schnackenburg, Festschrift A. Vögtle, Freiburg etc. 1975, p. 193.

the hands of men..." Jeremias observed that in the language of Jesus that involves a word-play: "The Son of Man will be delivered over to the sons of men," and that's *really* Jewish! But who will deliver "the Son of Man"? The gospels tell us that Judas delivered up Jesus to the Jewish priests; that the Jewish priests delivered up Jesus to Pilate; that Pilate delivered up Jesus to the soldiers for crucifixion. Interestingly, the early church came to see that ultimately it was God who delivered up Jesus for our sins (Romans 4:25, 8:32). There's no reason why Mark, and Jesus himself, shouldn't have seen both man and God in this action: in the last resort it was God who willed the death of Jesus, that mankind might find a place in his kingdom, but it was sinful men who were the unwitting instruments in bringing to pass God's purpose to overcome man's sin.

In each of the three prophecies of the death of Jesus it is *the Son of Man* who suffers, and is handed over to death and is to rise from death. This is not accidental, for the Son of Man is the representative of the kingdom of God (so Daniel 7:13), and his resurrection to the place of power is for rule in the kingdom of God. Here it is necessary to bring to focus various strands of thought in Judaism which throw light on this matter which has often been regarded as inexplicable from the Jewish standpoint. The Son of Man may be said to suffer: (1) as the Righteous Man, who is opposed by the unrighteous but who is vindicated by God's intervention; (2) as the Prophet of the End, the Bearer of the message of the kingdom, whose message is rejected by his contemporaries, but who is vindicated by God's bringing his word to pass; (3) as the Servant of the Lord, whose sufferings for others are accepted by God, and are followed by God's exaltation of him before the world; (4) as the Martyr for the truth of God, whose obedience to God culminates in a sacrifice for the guilty, but who is granted a place of honour. The tendency of recent years is for scholars to point to one or other of these figures in Jewish thought as providing the clue to the language of Jesus; it would seem that we need all of them to understand his teaching aright.

The idea of the Righteous Man who suffers at the hand of the unrighteous is deeply rooted in the Old Testament. It finds typical expression in Psalm 34:19:

> Many are the afflictions of the righteous man,
> but the Lord delivers him from them all.

It has been observed that the picture of the suffering Servant in Isaiah 53 links the thought of the suffering righteous man with that of the suffering rejected prophet. The fullest embodiment of the concept, however, is found in the Book of Wisdom, chapters 2 and 5. Two pictures are given of the righteous man, first in the words of evil men who determine to do away with him:

> Down with the poor and righteous man! Let us tread him under foot; let us show no mercy to the widow and no reverence for the gray hairs of old age. For us let might be right!...Let us lay a trap for the righteous man; he stands in our way, a check to us at every turn; he girds at us as law-breakers, and calls us traitors to our upbringing. He knows God, so he says; he calls himself "the servant of the Lord." He is a living condemnation of all our ideas. The very sight of him is an affliction to us, because his life is not like other people's, and his ways are different...He says that the righteous die happy, and boast that God is his father. Let us test the truth of his words, let us see what will happen to him in the end...Let us condemn him to a shameful death, for on his own showing he will have a protector.

The scene is removed to the judgment, where the wicked speak in a very different manner:

> Then the righteous man shall take his stand, full of assurance, to confront those who oppressed him and made light of all his sufferings; at the sight of him there will be terror and confusion, and they will be beside themselves to see him so unexpectedly safe home. Filled with remorse, groaning and gasping for breath, they will say among themselves:
>
> Was not this the man who was once our butt, a target for our contempt? Fools that we were, we held his way of life to be madness and his end dishonorable. To think that he is now counted one of the sons of God and assigned a place of his own among God's people! How far we strayed from the road of truth!

There is much else in the same strain. The simple pattern of Psalm 34:19 has been adapted to the understanding of resurrection, judgment and the kingdom of God, which the later prophets and apocalyptists opened up. It comes to completest expression in the saying of Jesus before the Sanhedrin: faced by the Jewish leaders bent on his destruction, and demanded to say whether he was the Messiah, he declared: "I am; and you shall see the son of Man sitting at the right hand of God, and coming with the clouds of heaven." The supremely righteous Man, persecuted unto death, is to be vindicated by God and revealed as the Lord of his persecutors. Comparison of the narratives of the sufferings, trial and death of Jesus in the gospels with writings like Wisdom 2-5 shows that the earliest Christians were conscious that Jesus fulfilled this pattern of the righteous man who suffers at the hands of the unrighteous, but is delivered by the intervention of God. This they will have learned from Jesus.

The concept of the prophet, rejected by his contemporaries but set in the right by God, was also in the mind of Jesus. For he himself called attention to the repetition in his ministry of the fate of the prophets of God. When told of Herod's desire to kill him, Jesus affirmed that he must continue on his way, because "it is unthinkable for a prophet to meet his death anywhere but in Jersusalem" (Luke 13:33). He cited the "wisdom of God," which told of the killing of prophets and righteous men from Abel to Zechariah, and the judgment which would be demanded of "this generation" for its wickedness in rejecting God's final Messenger (Matthew 23:34ff). He uttered a lament over Jerusalem as "the city which murders the prophets and stones the messengers sent to her" (Matthew 23:37). These passages form a crescendo of sayings, which indicate not only that Jerusalem and its people reject and kill prophets, but that Jesus himself was to add to the number of those so treated.

The suffering of the Servant of the Lord is related to both types of sufferers we have described, for he is a supreme example of the "righteous man" who endures suffering because of the unrighteous, and in the earlier Servant Songs he is depicted as a prophet, with a mission to restore Israel and bring light to the nations (Isaiah 49:2–6). There is likely to be a conscious link between the second passion prediction and the Servant Song of Isaiah 52:13–53:12, for the term "hand over," used in Mark 9:31 of the Son of Man, appears in Isaiah 53:12 and its equivalent in the Targum of Isaiah 53:5, and the notion of God handing over the Son of Man to die is especially close to Isaiah 53 (v. 10: "It was the Lord's will to crush him and cause him to suffer and...make his life a guilt offering"). Jesus himself is likely to have brought together these three figures of the suffering Righteous Man, the rejected Prophet, and the Servant of the Lord.

But what of the martyr? The pertinence of this figure has recently come to the attention of scholars. When the tyrant Antiochus Epiphanes in the second century B.C. attempted to destroy the religion of the Jews and force them to accept the religious practices of the pagan Greek world, he had no idea what a reaction he would provoke. The humble poor of Israel preferred to suffer torture unto death rather than renounce the faith of their fathers. From that time on it could be said, "The Jewish religion is a religion of martyrdom."[4] The martyr's fate and apocalyptic faith reacted on and stimulated on another: God's intervention for his people was eagerly anticipated, and with it the individual's participation in the kingdom of God through personal resurrection (Daniel 12:2). Moreover the sufferings of the martyr came to be viewed as having power to atone for the sins of the nation. The author of 4 Maccabees, who tells of the struggle of the Jews against Antiochus, concludes his story of the martyrs with this statement:

> Through them the enemy had no more power over our people, and the tyrant suffered punishment; and our country was purified, they having, as it were, become a ransom for our nation's sin; and through the blood of these righteous men and the propitiation of their death, the divine Providence delivered Israel that before was evil entreated (17:20ff).

With thought of this kind as part of his people's heritage it is not difficult to see how one, namely Jesus, who knew himself to be charged with the task of bringing the kingdom of God to men, saw himself called to bring to fulfillment these intimations of the destiny of God's chosen vessels.

A single feature of Jesus' language points this up: the Son of Man, he said, is to rise "after three days." Jewish teachers noticed how that phrase, or its equivalent "on the third day," appears frequently in scripture. In the Midrash on Genesis 42:17 a famous comment occurs: "The Holy One, blessed be

[4] *Die Religion des Judentums im späthellenistischen Zeitalter*, Tübingen 1926, p. 374.

he, never leaves the righteous in distress more than three days." The principle is illustrated at length from the scriptures in a comment on Genesis 22:4, where Abraham on the third day sees the place afar off where he was to offer Isaac, but where, of course, he was to experience a signal deliverance of God; in the tradition that place was viewed as the site of the temple, where sacrifices offered gained their value because of the sacrifice which Abraham virtually offered. Since all the other third day references relate to deliverances of various kinds, K. Lehmann concluded that "the third day" was not simply an expression for a short time, but a time stamped with special meaning:

> The third day brings the turning to something new and better. God's mercy and righteousness creates a new "time" of salvation, of life, of victory; the third day brings a difficult circumstance from decision, through God's saving action, to a final solution which is creative of history.[5]

It will be seen how significant it is that this one who is to suffer and be delivered to death and raised on the third day is *the Son of Man*; for he who is raised on the third day is exalted with God and brings salvation for the whole world. The Son of Man is the Righteous man *par excellence*, the Prophet of the end who brings to completion the prophecies of the end, the Servant of the Lord who becomes "light" for the nations, the supreme Martyr for the cause of God's kingdom. The Son of Man gathers up all these types into one figure, to carry through their service at the end of the times as the high point of the process whereby the kingdom of God comes and men may share in that kingdom.

Here we see the answer to the question constantly asked by students of the gospels: "How can the Son of Man of Daniel's exalted vision be viewed as a humble and humiliated man, the subject of prophecies of rejection, suffering and death?" It was the question of John the Baptist in prison, and of Peter when he first heard Jesus speak about his sufferings. The answer of Jesus is clear. The Son of Man of Daniel 7 must be understood in the light of the righteous sufferer of the Psalms, the rejected prophets of the Bible, the Servant of the

---

[5] *Auferweckt am Dritten Tag nach der Schrift,* Quaestiones Disputatae, ed. K. Rahner and H. Schlier, vol. 38, Freiburg, 2nd ed. 1969, p. 181.

songs of Isaiah, and the martyrs who give their lives for God's glory and their people's deliverance. In this way we see the unity which holds together the sayings regarding the Son of Man in his ministry, the Son of Man in his death and resurrection, and the Son of Man in his *parousia* at the end: *the binding link is the service for the kingdom of God which the Son of Man is commissioned to achieve.* In humble service of God for man, in suffering unto death, in rising to life, and in *parousia* in glory he is the Mediator of the kingdom of God, representative of God and representative of man.

The most closely related saying in the gospels to the Lord's prophecies of the passion is Mark 10:45:

> The Son of Man came not to be served but to serve,
> and to give his life as a ransom for the many.

There is a similar but shorter saying preserved in Luke 22:27, in the context of the Last Supper:

> I am in the midst of you as one who serves.

There is some uncertainty as to how these two sayings are related. Howard Marshall thinks that Mark 10:45 followed Luke's saying as a comment on it.[6] Schürmann, in a lengthy study on the Last Supper in Luke, suggested that Jesus spoke the sentence in Luke 22:27, and Mark conjoined it with an independent saying, thus:

> I am in the midst of you as one who serves;
> the Son of Man came to give his life a ransom for many.[7]

It could be that an original saying lay behind its two versions:

> The Son of Man...
> who serves,
> and gives his life
> a ransom for many.

That would form a perfect basis for the version of the saying given in 1 Timothy 2:6:

> (There is one Mediator between God and man)
> the man Christ Jesus,

---

[6] *Commentary on Luke,* New International Greek Testament Commentary, Exeter 1978, pp. 813-4.
[7] *Jesu Abschiedsrede, Lk. 22:21–38,* Münster 1967, p. 91.

who gave himself
a ransom for all.

Such discussions are admittedly inconclusive. The important factor is the setting forth of the Lord's death as a "ransom" for the race. Like the passion predictions, the saying gathers into one those intimations in the faith of Israel that acknowledge the redemptive power that death can have, especially the death of the martyrs and the Servant of the Lord, and above all of the last. It has often been pointed out that Mark 10:45 is closely parallel to Isaiah 53:10: "When thou shalt make his soul *an offering for sin...*," and the last clause of Song: "He *bore the sin of many,* and made intercession for the transgressors." It would be difficult to find any passage in Jewish literature so close to Mark 10:45 as that passage. Especially it should be noted that the sacrifice of the Servant in Isaiah 53:12 is for "many," for "the transgressors"; it is generally agreed "many" here denotes "all," as in the first stanza of the Song:

Just as there were many who were appalled at him...
so will he startle many nations (52:15).

The Servant stands as the one for the many, he offers himself for the life of *all*. No statement of Jews about the sacrifice made by the martyrs ever has such a thought in view. The fundamental idea is perhaps to be sought in the understanding of redemption as a new Exodus. At the first Exodus a lamb was sacrificed for each Israelite family, and the tribes were "redeemed," i.e. emancipated from slavery to become the free people of God in a new land. So through the offering of Jesus the Son of Man there is brought about an emancipation of all mankind, that all peoples may enter the promised land of the kingdom of God. Self-evidently that sacrifice has to be on behalf of all, for the kingdom of God is over all and for all; nothing less than a death that embraces all mankind in its power can bring about a kingdom which is destined to embrace the whole world.

This is the presupposition of the words and actions of Jesus in the Last Supper. Whether or not the meal was literally a passover celebration, as I believe it was, or an anticipated passover, as some consider, one thing is clear: the meal was filled with passover associations, and had in view that meal to which the passover in the days of Jesus pointed: the feast of the kingdom of God. Luke tells us that Jesus emphasized this point *twice* in the meal:

> I have eagerly desired to eat this Passover with you before I suffer. For I tell you, I will not eat it again until it finds fulfillment in the kingdom of God.

And again:

> After taking the cup he gave thanks, and said,
> Take this and divide it among you. For I tell you, I will not drink again of the fruit of the vine until the kingdom of God comes (Luke 22:15–18).

It was the duty of the one presiding at the passover meal to declare its meaning, and so to recall the first celebration at the Exodus and its continual signficance. Jesus added two unique features to its meaning as he conducted it. When he was about to hand round the bread at the beginning of the meal he broke the loaf and said, "This is my body." After the meal had finished he took the cup, and on handing it to the disciples said, "This is my blood of the new covenant." These actions provided a double parable of his sacrifice. On this we may affirm the following:

(i) Jesus himself did not eat the bread he gave, or drink from the cup he passed to his disciples, but he looked forward to eating and drinking in the meal which the Last Supper anticipated; i.e. in the feast of the Kingdom of God. The Last Supper is an anticipation of that feast, made possible by the sacrifice he was about to offer.

(ii) The use of the bread and wine recalls the acts of prophetic symbolism recorded in the Old Testament. The disciples were in so confused a state, they could scarcely take in the meaning of what Jesus was saying and doing; but two things they could not forget: he took the bread, and said it was his body, and when he handed them the cup he said it was his blood, given for them and for the world. As they later pondered these things they were able at length to grasp their meaning.

(iii) Jesus spoke of the necessity of his death for participation in the kingdom of God. The words "my blood of the (new) covenant" recall two Old Testament statements: Exodus 24:8, when Moses at the first Exodus sprinkled the people with blood and said, "See, the blood of the covenant"; Jeremiah 31:31, which announced the making of a new covenant, for the transformation of God's people to be the people of the kingdom of God. Observe carefully: the new covenant is not simply for the granting of the forgiveness of sins, but to reconstitute a people who should inherit the kingdom of God. The goal is a renewed people for the new age of the kingdom.

(iv) The giving of the bread and wine to the disciples were signs of Jesus' gift to them of a part in the benefits of his body given and blood shed; they were thereby assured of inclusion in the covenant and a place in the kingdom of God.

(v) This interpretation is made explicit in words which Luke alone has reserved:

> I appoint unto you in covenant the kingdom,
> as my Father has appointed it unto me in covenant,
> that you may eat and drink at my table in my kingdom,
> judging the twelve tribes of Israel.[8]

The application of these words is made first to the men sitting round the table with Jesus, but their wider meaning is apparent: receiving the bread and wine signified participation in the covenant for the kingdom through the death of the Lord who brings the kingdom, and that covenant has in view all who call upon the name of the Lord, since the blood was shed for "the many."

All this makes sense on the basis of one presupposition: the One who gives his body and blood, that man may enter the kingdom of God, passes from death to resurrection life, to return in power and glory as Lord of the kingdom of God. So surely as he was host at the feast which anticipates the coming of the kingdom of God, so surely will he preside at the feast which celebrates its coming at the end.

Conclusion

In relating the death and resurrection of Jesus to his

---

[8] The translation of Luke 22:29–30 by R. Otto, *Kingdom of God and Son of Man*, London 1938, p. 274, who rightly draws attention to the use of *diatithemai* in the making of a covenant.

teaching on the kingdom of God we are in touch with the fundamental meaning of the life and work of Jesus as he himself made it known. It is inexplicable that the Church through the centuries has so frequently ignored this aspect of the saving work of its Lord. Doubtless it is bound up with a failure to understand the Lord's teaching on the kingdom of God as God's royal, gracious and powerful action for salvation. The new covenant of God through the redemptive action of Christ is for life under his saving sovereignty; that life is experienced from the time that one acknowledges Jesus as Lord, and it looks for its fulness in the resurrection with Christ in his perfected kingdom. This is positive, powerful, and wonderful news for the world. We do well to proclaim it in its completeness.

CHAPTER FOUR

THE COMING OF GOD IN THE FUTURE COMING OF JESUS

The simple term "coming," when used in the New Testament of the coming of Christ in the power and glory of the final kingdom, has a very interesting equivalent in the Greek New Testament: it is the term *parousia*. Scholars like to use that word when talking about the coming of Christ at the end of the age, for it was stamped with a special meaning in the period of the early Christians. *Parousia* literally means "presence," and Paul sometimes used the word in that sense (as when he appealed to the Philippian Christians to be obedient not only in his *presence,* but still more in his *absence* from them – Philippians 2:12). But the term came to mean "coming so as to be present," and it was applied quite explicitly to the state visit of an eminent person, above all of the emperor himself. The *parousia* of an emperor to a city was a tremendous affair in the ancient world, and caused great excitement. Intense preparations were made for the occasion, not unlike what happens nowadays when an international fair is held in a city. The city would be cleaned up, special buildings would be erected and coins would be issued to commemorate the event, which would mark a new era from which future dates would be reckoned. Adolf Deissmann called attention to an inscription relating to the visit of the emperor Hadrian to Tegea in Greece; it was dated "in the year 69 of the first *parousia* of the god Hadrian to Greece." How interesting that 69 years after the event took place it was still remembered! That *parousia* had caused a new beginning of the dating of the years for the country. Strangely, it was about that time when Christians began to talk about the first *parousia* of Christ in distinction from his second *parousia*. In a papyrus letter from Egypt some peasants addressed a high ranking official with the words, "It is a subject of prayer with us night and day to be held worthy of your welcome *parousia*," and they added that they look for him "as they watch eagerly from Hades for the future *parousia* of Christ the everlasting God."[1] Here the *parousia* of a ruler and the *parousia* of Christ are placed side by side. Evidently the word was a favourite one with early Christians, and it gained a special meaning through its contemporary use in such contexts. We do not have a modern English equivalent for it; somehow the "State Visit of the Lord Jesus" does not sound right to represent the coming of our Lord in power and glory! So perhaps we may use the term *parousia* on occasion, remembering its special meaning.

Parousia is a Greek word, and Jesus normally spoke Aramaic. How did he refer to the event in view? Strangely, Jesus never actually used the expression "my coming" of his future advent, but he used a mode of speech that was by no means clear to everybody who heard him speak. When he did not refer to his advent by means of parables (like "The Thief in the Night") he always spoke about *the coming of the Son of Man*. There is a discourse about this in Luke 17:22ff, where Jesus talks of "the day of the Son of Man". The Son of Man in his day will be like the lightning flash (Luke 17:24); the day when the Son of Man is revealed will be like the day when Noah went into the ark and the flood came (vv. 26f); it will be like the day when Lot went out of Sodom and destruction came upon the city (vv. 28f). The discourse of Mark 13 reaches its climax in a description of this event:

> They will see the Son of Man coming in the clouds with great power and glory, and he will send out the angels and gather his chosen from the four winds, from the farthest bounds of earth to the farthest bounds of heaven.

And Jesus told the High Priest and his court:

---

[1] *Light from the Ancient East,* London 1910, pp. 377-8 (the discussion on the term parousia is on pp. 372-8).

You will see the Son of Man seated at the right hand of God, and coming with the clouds of heaven (Mark 14:62).

Why did Jesus use this language about the Son of Man? Why did he not speak plainly of his own coming? Possibly there was more than one reason. In the first place he was alluding to a scripture passage to which he evidently attached great importance, namely Daniel 7:13. In that chapter the kingdoms of this world are represented in visionary and symbolic form as beasts from the sea, and they reach their climax in a monster which tramples the earth and wages war on the saints of God. God then comes with his court in order to pass judgment on the monster and stop his rampaging. The beast is killed, and his carcass destroyed. We then read:

> I saw one like a son of man coming with the clouds of heaven; he approached the Ancient in Years and was presented before him. Sovereignty and glory and kingly power were given to him, so that all people and nations of every language should serve him; his sovereignty was to be an everlasting sovereignty which should not pass away, and his kingdom one that should not be destroyed.

When Jesus spoke about the coming of the Son of Man he had that passage in view; the coming was for the bringing to victory of the rule of God among men. The symbolism of the vision in Daniel favours the belief that the "one like a son of man" was himself the one who, at God's behest, brought to an end the power of the antigod monster, and so delivered God's people and opened the way for the kingdom to come. This is close to the heart of Jesus' teaching on the rôle of the Son of Man in the kingdom of God.

The second reason why Jesus used this language about the Son of Man is bound up with the meaning and use of expression. "Son of Man" is a typically Semitic way of referring to a member of the human race. In Hebrew the same kind of language was used regarding animals, so that one could speak about a "son of cattle," meaning a calf or a heifer, or a "son of a dove" as a single male dove," and even a "son of a racing mare" for a fast running horse.[2] So "son of man" means a man. It now seems established, in the light of re-

---

[2] See the article of G. Fohrer in Kittel's *Theological Dictionary of the New Testament*, vol. VIII, pp. 346f.

searches by G. Vermes and J. Jeremias, that in Galilean Aramaic it was possible for a speaker to make statements about the Son of Man when he really meant himself.[3] We can do something similar in English by using the third person pronoun "one." for example, I could say, with reference to some particular statement, "One would hardly put the matter that way," when what I really meant was, "I wouldn't say it like that." Vermes has pointed out two important aspects of this use: first, this way of using the expression "son of man" for oneself was prompted through a speaker wishing to avoid undue or immodest emphasis on himself, or through fear or dislike of asserting openly something disagreeable to himself (plus a few other motives not relevant to our inquiry); secondly, it made it possible for a speaker to make statements which could refer to himself, or to another, or even to man in general, and reflection had to be used to discover just what was intended.

Let me recount one of the examples of this latter use cited by Vermes. Rabbi Simeon ben Yohai is said to have hidden for thirteen years in a cave during the reign of Hadrian:

> At the end of those thirteen years he said, I will go forth to see what is happening in the world. He then went forth and sat at the entrance to the cave. There he saw a hunter trying to catch birds by spreading his net. He heard a heavenly voice saying, "Release," and the bird escaped. He then said, "Not even a bird perishes without the will of heaven. How much less the son of man" (1 Sheb. 38d).

The story is repeated in Genesis Rabba 79:6 with a slightly different ending:

> Not even a bird is caught without the will of heaven. How much less the soul of the son of man. So he went forth and found that affairs had quietened down.

There is one manuscript of this latter version in which "the soul of the son of man" is replaced by "my soul": "Not even a bird is caught without the will of heaven. How much less my soul."[4]

---

[3] For Jeremias, see his discussion on Son of Man in his *New Testament Theology*, London 1971, pp. 258-276. Vermes' findings are most easily seen in his book *Jesus the Jew*, New York 1973, pp. 160-191.

[4] Vermes, *op. cit.* p. 167

When one ponders the implications of that use of "son of man," ambiguous, yet evidently used of the speaker himself, one cannot help thinking of sayings in which Jesus spoke about the Son of Man. Consider for example the following:

> Foxes have their holes, the birds their nests, but the Son of Man has nowhere to lay his head (Matthew 8:20).
>
> John came, neither eating nor drinking, and they say, "He is possessed." The Son of Man came eating and drinking, and they say, "Look at him! A glutton and a drinker, a friend of tax-gatherers and sinners" (Matthew 11:19f).
>
> The Sabbath was made for man, and not man for Sabbath; therefore the Son of Man is sovereign even over the Sabbath (Mark 2:28).
>
> Everyone who acknowledges me before men, the Son of Man will acknowledge before the angels of God; but he who disowns me before men will be disowned before the angels of God (Luke 12:8).

The equivocal nature of these sayings is so complete, even modern exegetes still do not agree on who is in mind: man in general, Jesus, or (in the last case) some other individual. Nevertheless the ambiguity of the expression "Son of Man" in such passages agrees with the steadfast policy of Jesus not to make public statements of himself as the Messiah, yet at the same time so to relate himself to his mission for the kingdom of God that those with ears to hear and eyes to see could grasp the real meaning of what he was saying. This includes his statements about the necessity of the Son of Man's suffering for the cause of the kingdom of God, and those about the *parousia* of the Son of Man. In all these sayings which relate to the ministry of the Son of Man, to the suffering of the Son of Man, and to the *parousia* of the Son of Man, it is the same person who is in mind: that "one like a son of man" in Daniel's vision, through whom the cause of God comes to triumph and to whom the final rule of God is committed.

Of the many sayings relating to the coming of the Son of Man, one above all is of particular interest to our study, namely the utterance of Jesus before the Jewish court, which sought to formulate a charge against him that could be laid before the Roman governor, a charge of sufficient gravity to warrant the death penalty. Failing to gain from witnesses evidence suitable to this end, the High Priest tries his hand, in hope of eliciting from Jesus an incriminatory statement. He asks Jesus whether he is the Messiah, "the Son of the Blessed One." Jesus replies, "I am, and you will see the Son of Man seated at the right hand of the Power (i.e. God), and coming with the clouds of heaven." Now there are several features of this reply which we must consider.

On this occasion, as in all similar statements in the gospels, it is the Son of Man who comes with the clouds of heaven. Moreover here, as in other sayings that refer to the Son of Man coming for judgment, Jesus gives the impression of distinguishing between himself and the Son of Man. The High Priest asks, "Are *you* the Messiah?" Jesus replies, "*I am*, and you will see *the Son of Man* coming..." Theoretically it would be possible to maintain that Jesus here differentiates between the Messiah and the Son of Man who is to come in power. In the context of Jewish thinking, however, let alone that of Jesus himself, it is an impossible distinction to draw. For the Messiah is he who is coming to rule on God's behalf in the kingdom of God, and the Son of Man is he who is coming to rule on God's behalf in the kingdom of God. Jesus could not say in one breath (nor anyone else in his name): "I am in truth the Messiah who is to rule for God; and you will see another, the Son of Man, coming to rule for God." On the contrary, it is as clear as day in this saying that Jesus is both Messiah and the Son of Man who is to come for the final kingdom of God. The reason for his speaking in this manner is first to acknowledge that he is the Messiah, but then to define in what sense he is the Messiah: not simply a king from David's line, but the Lord at God's right hand of Psalm 110 and the coming Son of Man of Daniel's vision. The saying accordingly is the crucial place of identification of Jesus with the glorified Son of Man. Jesus knows that he will die for making the declaration, but declare it he must, for this is God's appointed destiny for him. This statement therefore throws light on every ambiguous passage about the Son of Man which has preceded it in the gospel: *the Son of Man is Jesus in his total ministry for the kingdom of God.*

The second feature to note is the link between this saying and those relating to the sufferings of the Son of Man. We have observed how the latter sayings succinctly sum up all that the Old Testament and contemporary Judaism said and thought about the Righteous Man who suffers, the Rejected Prophet, the Servant of the Lord, and the Martyrs for God. Inevitably these figures tend to merge into one another, for the righteous are often prophets to their people, the Servant of the Lord is a prophet-witness for God, and many such persons suffered the fate of the martyr. Now it is significant that in the literature of the period of Jesus there are frequent references to God's raising his suffering and martyred servants to his right hand. In the Testament of Job, Job tells the kings who lament over his sufferings that he has a throne among the holy ones in heaven:

> My throne is in the supra-terrestrial realm, and its splendour and majesty are from the right hand of the Father in the heavens.

In the Apocalypse of Elijah it is said of the martyrs:

> The Lord says: I shall place them at my right hand, they will render thanks for the others...they will receive the thrones of glory and crowns.

It is likely that this thinking was decisively affected by Psalm 110:1, where the king (Messiah) is told to sit at God's right hand till God makes his enemies his footstool; so also the martyrs for God's cause will be raised by God above their enemies to a position of honour in God's kingdom. Jesus went directly to that psalm, and declared that God would set him at his right hand, in the position of honour and authority. But in the utterance before the Sanhedrin Jesus goes beyond what any martyr anticipated for himself: as that one who is exalted to God's right hand, he will appear with the clouds of heaven to bring to victory God's rule over all who oppose it; and this he will do, since he is to be in the future what he is in the present – the representative of God's rule, and its mediator to the world.

So we find in this saying the whole complex of Jesus' teaching about the kingdom of God and the Son of Man brought to a climax: he who revealed the kingdom of God in action in humble service among the poor, and brought that service to its perfect expression in the obedient death on the cross, is exalted by God in resurrection to the place of power and glory; as the Lord of all authority and might he will bring to completion God's saving purpose for man, putting down its opponents, and bestowing its blessings on all who look to God for salvation. The High Priest did not misunderstand what Jesus said. To him this was a claim beyond anything that he and his compatriots made for the Messiah; to talk about being seated with God, and coming with the clouds of glory as God comes, exercising judgment over men, setting his enemies under his feet, and with it all rejecting the authority of Israel's High Priest and court and implying that even *they* would be judged by him in that day – this was more than their ears could endure; it was blasphemy, and it called for the appropriate judgment.

Before we leave this saying I would ask your patience to consider a further question. The High Priest, we say, did not misunderstand Jesus' words; did *the Church* misunderstand what Jesus said? If that sounds a strange question, it must be recognized that a number of scholars of recent times have believed that Jesus was misunderstood, both by the disciples and by the Church that followed them. They maintain that in the vision of Daniel 7, the Son of Man comes with the clouds of heaven to the Ancient of Days, and so *ascends* on the clouds to God in heaven, he does not *descend* from heaven to earth. This, they urge, Jesus would have recognized; accordingly his statement to the High Priest signified his conviction that he would be vindicated by God through resurrection in the immediate future; he had no thought of a coming from heaven to earth at some unknown time in the future. J. A. T. Robinson adopted this view; he maintained that the sitting at the right hand of God, spoken of in Psalm 110:1, and the coming with the clouds of heaven, described in Daniel 7;13, have the same fundamental meaning, namely God's vindication of Jesus. Asked when that should occur Robinson replied:

> There can be no doubt that it refers to the only moment to which all the enthronement language applied to Jesus does refer, namely to the moment of the resurrection onwards; for there is never a suggestion that Jesus enter upon his triumph only at some second coming.[5]

---

[5] *Jesus and his Coming, The Emergence of a Doctrine,* London 1957, p. 45.

That sounds very reasonable, and it makes one sit up and think. When, however, one ponders the issues, the improbability of this interpretation becomes evident.

Contrary to what is maintained, Daniel 7:13 does not describe an ascent to heaven of the one like a son of man. The vision adapts for its symbolism the ancient story of the conquest of the monster of the deep by a powerful god of heaven. In the ancient saga the one from heaven is a storm god, hence he rides on the clouds of heaven, and is frequently called the "cloud-rider." When the monster of the sea threatens to destroy the dwellers in heaven the storm god comes from heaven to fight the monster, and with his powerful weapons of the storm he destroys the evil power. This picture became a kind of standard cartoon in the Bible to represent evil political powers that act wickedly towards the people of God and are overthrown; in the Old Testament it was applied to Egypt in its oppression of Israel and its conquest by God, and in the Book of Revelation to the Roman empire in its blasphemous opposition to the gospel and Church of Christ. In Daniel's application of the cartoon, it is explicity stated that the Ancient of Days "came" for judgment with his court, i.e. he came to the scene of the monster's raging; the one like a son of man than "came" with the clouds of heaven to do the bidding of the Ancient of Days, and to receive the kingdom. The vision thus records a "theophany," i.e. a "coming" of God, and also of his representative. In the Bible without exception a theophany is always to the world, where the wicked engage in their rebellion, and where the saints suffer and need deliverance. There are no early Jewish writers on Daniel 7 who thought of the Son of Man coming to any other place than the earth, where the Messiah comes to rule for God.

That Jesus read the passage and used it in this manner is clear from one feature of his statement to the High Priest and his court: "*You shall see* the Son of Man sitting at the right hand of God and coming with the clouds..." There is no suggestion that by this Jesus meant that these men would see him in his risen glory in or after Easter, as Saul of Tarsus did; nor of their coming to perceive, by reason of the ongoing advance of the Church, that Jesus was the exalted Messiah. Jesus meant that these men would see him in the kind of events described in Daniel's vision: himself installed by God as lord of the world, and coming on God's behalf to carry through the judgment and establish in power the rule of God; in that event the Jewish leaders would experience a reversal of the present situation, in that they would be the condemned and Jesus the Judge and Lord of the kingdom. The disciples did not misunderstand Jesus, nor the evangelists misinterpret him, nor the Church misconstrue what Jesus meant. There is a crystal clarity about the statement in Mark 14:62, and it provides the key to the rest of our Lord's sayings on this theme.

The description of the *parousia* of the Son of Man in Mark 13:24–27 is closely related to the statement of Jesus at his trial. It forms the point to which the discourse moves, and the centre from which its conclusion proceeds. It is distinguished however by its description of "cosmic" signs, i.e. terrifying happenings in the heavens, which precede and accompany the coming of the Son of Man:

> The sun will be darkened, the moon will not give her light;
> the stars will come falling from the sky,
> the celestial powers will be shaken.
> Then they will see the Son of Man coming in the clouds
> with great power and glory.

This passage is very important, since it links the coming of the Son of Man with the representations of the coming of God on the Day of the Lord which form the heart of the Old Testament hope for the future. Various Old Testament passages are alluded to in vv. 24-25, above all Isaiah 13:10, 34:4 and Joel 2:10, 4:15–16. The term with which v. 25 concludes (the celestial powers *will be shaken*) does not occur in those passages, but it is a standard term in Old Testament descriptions of theophany (e.g. Judges 5:5, Amos 9:5, Micah 1:4, Habakkuk 3:6, Nahum 1:5). A dozen other texts than those alluded to in vv. 24-25 would have done equally well to express the idea in mind. The important thing is that Jesus spoke of his *parousia* in terms of the theophany of the Lord. Somehow this seems to have escaped the majority of exegetes on the gospels, for they will keep on expounding this passage as though it has in mind the break up of the universe. For example, a noted writer on the Son of Man in the teaching of Jesus, H. E. Tödt, writes of our passage:

At the very moment when the earth is dissolving amidst cosmic convulsions, the Son of Man shows himself with great power and glory and commands his angels to rescue his elect from the desolation.[6]

This is far removed from what the Old Testament prophets and poets had in mind when they spoke of the coming of God. If we compare the passage with the description of the Day of the Lord in Isaiah 34 and the picture of the coming of God in Habakkuk 3, we will see at once what those writers had in mind: the heavens above and the earth beneath are in terror and confusion before the overwhelming might of the Lord of Heaven when he steps forth in judgment and salvation. None of the descriptions of theophany in the Old Testament envisages the destruction of the universe at the coming of God, rather they highlight the glory of the coming of the Lord when he moves to set right the wrongs of earth and establish righteousness and peace among the nations. So also the intention of Mark 13:24–27 is to focus on the glory of the coming of the Son of Man and to put it in its proper category: it represents the intervention of God for judgment and salvation.

It may further be observed that the setting of the *parousia* in the context of cosmic phenomena in Mark 13:24–25 indicates the indescribable nature of that event. Descriptions of the confusion of sun, moon and stars in connection with a theophany are part of a long standing imagery, which conveyed the notion of the power and majesty of God when he acts to establish his will in the world. The coming of God in the clouds of heaven belongs to that same tradition. Accordingly the portrayal of the *parousia* of the Son of Man in terms of coming on the clouds of heaven must be similarly understood. The form of the portrayal forbids our interpreting it as a literal description of the event. There is, admittedly, one feature in descriptions of the *parousia* which represents an advance beyond Old Testament statements about theophany: mention is made of the "revelation" of the Son of Man on that day (Luke 17:30). The early Church therefore often spoke of

---

[6] *The Son of Man in the synoptic Tradition*, London 1965, p. 34.

the *parousia* as the "revelation" of the Lord Jesus (e.g. 1 Corinthians 1:7) or as his "appearing' (e.g. 2 Timothy 4:8). Even so the *how* of this action and revelation of hidden glory is not deducible from the pictorial descriptions of it, as Revelation 19:11–16 clearly illustrates. These things belong to the mystery of God's final work in the world of man. Paul said in a related context, "the day will declare it" (1 Corinthians 3:13). That day we may anticipate with wonder, joy and hope.

Perhaps it should be mentioned that no word about the judgment which the Son of Man may exercise is mentioned in our passage; it simply speaks of his gathering his elect "from the end of earth to the end of heaven." Who are these "elect"? In Mark 13:20 the elect are the godly of Israel who suffer in the tribulation linked with the destruction of Jerusalem, but no such limitation is likely in our passage. Zechariah 2:6 is one of the passages alluded to in the gathering of the elect of v. 27; that verse is soon followed by the remarkable statement of Zechariah 2:11:

> Many nations shall come over to the Lord on that day and become his people, and he will make his dwelling with you.

The unity of Gentiles and Jews in one people of the kingdom of God is a highly unusual expectation in the Old Testament. That Jesus himself looked for Gentiles to stream from the ends of the earth into the kingdom of God, while "sons of the kingdom" would be exluded, is evident from Matthew 8:11ff. The universal implications of Mark 13:27 could well assume the gathering of the elect of all nations, along with the penitents of Israel, into a single community under the lordship of Christ. That would form a fitting climax to the description of the coming of the Son of Man.

Mark 13:24–27 forms the climax of a forecast of the future, precipitated by a prophecy of Jesus relating to the destruction of the temple of Jerusalem. "Not one stone will be left upon another," he said, "all will be thrown down" (Mark 13:2). Sayings of Jesus relating to the future are brought together to elucidate the implications of that prophecy. Warnings of troubles in the world and distress for his followers are followed by statements about the tribulation which will fall on Jerusalem and its people. We must be quite clear that there is no justification for believing that what Jesus says in this context relates to a time far distant from his earthly ministry. The "stones" of the temple that will be thrown down are of the building which Jesus was at that moment leaving, and the distress of Israel which he decribed was of the generation to which he and his disciples belonged. This becomes plain from other related sayings of our Lord. He had earlier stated that the innocent blood spilt from the murder of Abel in Genesis to that of Zechariah, described in 2 Chronicles 24:20:22, and so from the beginning to the end of the Bible, would be visited on "this generation"; for it not only continued to reject the messengers of God, but was guilty of refusing the ultimate Apostle of God, Jesus the Christ. "Go on then," said Jesus, "finish off what your fathers began. This generation will bear the guilt of it all" (Matthew 23:32). In this passage, as in Mark 13:14ff, Jesus was declaring judgment upon Israel, in a similar manner as earlier prophets had foretold the coming of the Day of the Lord upon the nation. Jesus thus was foretelling a Day of the Lord upon Jerusalem and its people; and it was to this that Jesus referred when he said, "This generation shall not pass till all this be fulfilled" (Mark 13:30). These words are almost identical with those which are recorded in Matthew 23:36, relating to the judgment for rejecting the prophets and the Messiah: "Amen, I tell you, all these things shall come upon this generation." Mark's setting of the statement in its present position, close to the description of the coming of the Son of Man, has undoubtedly caused confusion to many modern believers, who stand at a distance from the tribulation of Israel in AD 70. Yet Mark has given to us another saying of Jesus, relating to the parousia, which ought to enable us to see the distinction Jesus drew between the Day of the Lord on Jerusalem and the coming of the Son of Man: "About that day or that hour no one knows, neither the angels in heaven, nor even the Son, but only the Father" (Mark 13:32). Those scholars are surely right who regard this saying as a cornerstone of the eschatological teaching of Jesus. We must fit other statements in relation to it, and not subordinate it to other lesser sayings. And the reason for this is the underlying attitude expressed in the saying: neither man, nor angel, nor even the Son of Man knows the time of the end; only the Father knows that, because he alone determines the time of the judgment and the kingdom; and so Jesus has taught us that the determination of the last time is "the exclusive reserve of the Majesty of God."[7] Significantly the same thing is implied in an utterance from the risen Lord preserved by Luke in Acts 1:7: "It is not for you to know the times and seasons which the Father has set in his own authority." But Mark 13:32 goes one stage further: it is the part of the Son to leave them in the Father's hands, for the mark of the Son is to maintain complete obeidence to the Father. Would that the followers of the Son had shown the same meekness and obedience regarding the time of the end, and that his followers today would do the same! For all attempts to declare the date of the coming of the Lord are erroneous, and manifest the pride of disobedience to the Father.

It remains to be said that this same attitude of Jesus to the unknowability of the time of the end is expressed in many other passages of his teaching, and it issues in warnings and appeals to be ready for the coming of the Lord, since we can never know just when it will be. This is seen in his parables, the Thief in the Night (Matthew 24:42ff), the Wise and Foolish Maidens (Matthew 25:1–13) and the Talents (Matthew 25:14–30). His comparison of the day of the Son of Man with conditions in the days of Noah and of Lot have a similar lesson: the coming will be like a lightning flash, therefore sudden and incalculable, and it will overtake many unawares, like the judgments upon the careless generation of Noah and the people of Sodom. "Watch! Keep spiritually alert!" is a keynote of our Lord's teaching (Mark 13:33–37). Not that he wanted us to scan anxiously the skies at all times; we remember the words of the angel to the disciples who were doing that (Acts 1:11). Pierre Bonnard, in his commentary on Matthew, points out that the meaning of the sentence which concludes the parable of the Wise and Foolish

---

[7] A. Vögtle, *Exegetische Erwägungen über das Wissen und Selbstbewusstsein Jesu*, in *Gott und Welt*, Festschrift K. Rahner, Freiburg 1964, vol. 1, p. 651.

Maidens, "Watch, for you do not know the day or the hour", (v. 13) is embodied in the two parables which follow: it is fulfilled as we carry out the mission committed to us by the Lord (as in the parable of the Talents), and as we go to the aid of the least of the brothers of the Son of Man in their need (as in the parable of the Sheep and Goats). Spiritual alertness, therefore, expresses itself in service for Christ in the world.[8]

There is thus immense challenge in the doctrine of the *parousia*, as well as great encouragement. The encouragement lies in the assurance that the Lord will bring to pass that purpose for which creation was made, and in that purpose we who belong to him are to have a part. The challenge lies in the call to live and serve in a manner that befits those who possess so wonderful a prospect.

This latter point is illustrated in a parable of peculiar intensity told by Jesus. He told of a widow who asked a judge to set right an injustice which she suffered. At first he refused, but in the end he did what she wanted, solely to save his reputation. Jesus drew the lesson:

> You hear what the unrighteous judge says. And will not God vindicate his chosen, who cry out to him day and night, while he exercises patience with them? I tell you, he will vindicate them soon enough. But when the Son of Man comes, will he find faith on earth? (Luke 18:6–8)

The last question is extraordinary. It cannot ask whether the Christian faith will still exist on earth when the Lord comes. Rather the faith in view is that which the woman in the story exemplifies, and which was so inconspicuous in the Israel of Jesus' time: a faith which acknowledges Jesus as the Son of Man, Saviour and Lord of the coming kingdom; a faith which prompts the earnest cry to God that he may send his Christ and with him the promised kingdom; a faith which burns brightly even when the elect are called to suffer as the Son of Man suffered; a faith which faithfully serves even while waiting. Whether the Son of Man will find that sort of faith in his coming has to be answered by each of us. The least that we can say will be, "Yes, Lord, when you come you'll find it in *me!*"

---

[8] *L'évangile selon Matthieu*, Neuchâtel and Paris, 2nd ed. 1970, pp. 358-9.

We conclude this study of the Lord and the kingdom of God with a question related to our observation at the end of chapter 2: what are the implications of this study concerning our understanding of Jesus?

We saw that the Old Testament looked forward to the coming of God to establish judgment and justice on the earth, and so to fulfill his purpose in creation through a world-embracing salvation. That promised saving sovereignty we saw initiated in and through the ministry of Jesus. He was the instrument and mediator of the kingdom of God in history. Moreover, he taught that this service for the kingdom of God was to reach a climax in his death and resurrection, by which God's saving rule would be made effective and available for all the world. He described the coming of the Son of Man at the end of the age, with power to judge and to rule, implying that his mediation of the saving rule of God is complete, for he not only initiates it but fulfills it, in the end and in the way God has determined. This mediation includes entry into or exclusion from the kingdom of God, as Luke 12:8f and Mark 8:38 narrate:

> Everyone who confesses me before men
> the Son of Man will confess,
> when he comes in the glory of his Father with the holy angels.
>
> Everyone who denies me before men
> the son of Man will deny,
> when he comes in the glory of his Father with the holy angels.[9]

Response to the word of God through Jesus is thus determinative for entry into the kingdom of God. The verdict of the Son of Man is identical with that of God. As the mediator of the kingdom of God Jesus occupies a unique position: as Son of Man he stands with man as man's representative before God; and as Son of Man he stands with God as representative of God's rule to man. The unparalleled nature of the relation of Jesus as Son of Man to God is indicated by the mode of his parousia: he comes *with the clouds of heaven,* and

---

[9] So W. G. Kümmel reconstructs the original version of the saying, see his article *Das Verhalten Jesus gegenuber und das Verhalten des Menschensohns, Markus 8:38 par und Lukas 12. 8f par,* in *Jesus und der Menschensohn,* pp. 216-9 (see the whole article, pp. 210-224).

so reveals God's acts in God's ways and in God's glory.

There is no category known to man in which Jesus can be placed. "Messiah" only dimly describes the reality, unless one fills the term with the attributes of the risen, exalted and returning Lord. He stands with man, sharing the attributes of man; and he stands with God, sharing the attributes of God.

We understand why it is recorded in the Fourth Gospel: "I and the Father are one" (John 10:30).

www.ingramcontent.com/pod-product-compliance
Lightning Source LLC
LaVergne TN
LVHW021624080426
835510LV00019B/2744